I SPY With My Little Eye... St. Patrick's Day

Let's Play

I Spy

Saint Patrick's Day

Can you spot

everything?

I spy with my little eye, something beginning with ...

L is for...

Leprechaun!

I spy with my little eye,
5 leprechauns ...

Leprechauns

I spy with my little eye, something beginning with ...

is for...
Dog!

I spy with my little eye, something beginning with ...

is for...

Glove!

I spy with my little eye, something beginning with ...

is for...

Coins!

I spy with my little eye, something red ...

The Hearts

Are Red

I spy with my little eye, something beginning with ...

is for...

Harp!

I spy with my little eye, something beginning with ...

is for...
Balloon!

I spy with my little eye,
7 green stars ...

2
1
3
4
5
6
7
Green Stars

I spy with my little eye, something beginning with ...

P is for... Pot of gold!

I spy with my little eye, 3 girls with hats ...

Girls with Hats

I spy with my little eye, something orange ...

The Fox

Is Orange

I spy with my little eye, something beginning with ...

is for...
Rainbow!

I spy with my little eye, something beginning with ...

is for...

Owl!

I spy with my little eye,
5 hearts ...

Hearts

I spy with my little eye, something beginning with ...

T is for... Tree!

I spy with my little eye, something beginning with ...

S

is for...
Socks!

I spy with my little eye, something yellow ...

The Horseshoe

Is Yellow

I spy with my little eye, something beginning with ...

F is for ... Flag

Did You Enjoy This I Spy Saint Patrick's Day Book?
Then check out our other kids activity books or leave a review!
Thank you for your support!

Made in the USA
Coppell, TX
15 March 2020